Blockchain Technology & Blueprint Ultimate Guide:

Learn Everything You Need to Know

For Beginners & Experienced

Contents

Introduction

Most of us have heard of Bitcoin but how many of us are aware of the technology that underlies it – the blockchain. The blockchain is one of the most forward-thinking crypto technologies of today's digital world. While it started life as the backbone for Bitcoin, the blockchain has gone on to become the technology of choice for any decentralized, distributed consensus system.

The blockchain itself is nothing more than a public ledger, a ledger of transactions that is so transparent, everyone can see what is going on, every step of the way. We all know about authentication, especially on the internet. We all have to use passwords to sign in, we all have to prove who we are when we do something or pay for something and each of these activities is regulated by a central system. Think of your bank account; your salary goes in, your bills are paid by a debit system and your account is maintained, accessible online or in a bank. All of this is regulated by a financial services authority, in this case, your bank, and everything you do is monitored and tracked electronically. Everything is kept confidential and secure but someone else still has control of your money.

With the blockchain, while every transaction is secure and confidential, the only person that has any control is you and you alone. The blockchain also solves another problem – with centralized systems, it costs money and the transactions take time. With the blockchain, each transaction costs a tiny fraction of what a centralized system would charge and each transaction is instant. You can send money from one side of the world to the other in a split second and, while you can already do this with services like PayPal, the costs of the blockchain are much lower.

Throughout this book, you will become familiar with blockchain. We will be looking at the concepts that keep it secure, such as public and private keys, digital signatures and hashing. We will be looking at how the blockchain is kept secure, the technology that underlies it, making it one of the most trusted systems in the world, safe from malicious users and with no chance of being hacked.

We are going to look at what the blockchain could be used for in the future and what it is used for now; we take a look at the most famous use case of the blockchain – Bitcoin, and what makes it tick, how it all works. And we are going to take a look at how blockchain is going to change the world, the financial world, as we know it.

The blockchain is not a simple ledger although what you see when you look at it may look simple. It is complex, full of algorithms, checking mechanisms to ensure security and it goes much deeper and much further than any other financial system. By the end of this book, you will be well-versed in what blockchain is and what it does, how it operates and, perhaps more importantly, why it works so well, why so many governments and financial institutions are likely to take up the use of the blockchain in the near future. Even more importantly, you will have an understanding of how blockchain can benefit you and your future!

Chapter 1: Cryptography

What is cryptography? It is an ancient art, one of codes, of secret writing, we've all seen the spy movies, some of us will even have written is secret code when we were younger. But the very first use of cryptography can be documented back to around 1900 BC, when non-standard hieroglyphs were used in an inscription by a scribe. There are those who argue the art of cryptography was a spontaneous result of the invention of writing, with uses from diplomatic messages to battle plans. It shouldn't come as any surprise to know that a new form of cryptography appeared after computer communication became more widespread. Let's face it, we should all know that, if we are communicating across a medium that is not trusted, we need some form of cryptography to keep what we are doing private and secure.

Today, cryptography is used for five main functions:

1. **Privacy and Confidentiality -** To ensure that only the intended recipient can read a message.

2. **Authentication** – to prove your identity
3. **Integrity** – to reassure the recipient that the message is exactly as you sent it and has not been changed.
4. **Non-repudiation** – a mechanism put in place to prove that you sent the message and it hasn't been intercepted.
5. **Key Exchange** – the way in which cryptography keys are shared between the sender and the recipient.

Cryptography always begins with plaintext data, data that is unencrypted. This is encrypted and becomes ciphertext and this will be unencrypted back to plain text. This encryption/decryption is always based on a key and on the cryptography scheme in use.

$C = E_k(P)$
$P = D_k(C)$

In this formula:

- P is plaintext

- C is ciphertext

- E is the encryption method used

- D is the decryption method used

- K is the key

Three terms that you will come across and that you must NOT confuse are:

- **Cryptography** – the encryption/decryption of messages through mathematical algorithms

- **Cryptanalysis** – the analyses and breaking of the encryption schemes

- **Cryptology** – Covering both above, this is the study of secret writing

3 Cryptographic Algorithms

There are several ways for cryptographic algorithms to be classified and these are the three most common ways, based on how many keys are used for the encryption/decryption and by their use and application:

- **SKC – Secret Key Cryptography –** a single key is used for encryption and decryption – often known as symmetric encryption and is used for confidentiality and privacy

- **PKC – Public Key Cryptography –** separate keys are used for encryption and decryption – often known as asymmetric encryption and is used mostly for key exchange, non-repudiation and authentication purposes

- **Hash Functions –** these encrypt information irreversibly using mathematical transformations, providing a kind of digital fingerprint. These are usually used for proving integrity of messages

Basic Principles of Cryptography

There are four basic principles of cryptography:

1. **Encryption**

Simply put, encryption is all about converting data into a form that is not readable by the human eye. This protects our privacy while the message is sent between two people. The recipient gets the decrypted version of the message that is encrypted when the sender sends it. Encryption and decryption require the use of a key, sometimes the same key, although usually different keys are required.

2. Authentication

Authentication is what makes sure the message comes from who it claims to come from. Let's say that Alice sends Bob a message; Bob wants to know that the message really came from Alice. Alice can perform an action on the message that Bob knows only she can do – that is the fundamental basis of authentication.

3. Integrity

One of the biggest issues faced by communication systems is a loss of integrity from messages that are being sent between people. Use of a cryptographic hash ensures that the messages are not intercepted and changed along the path of communication.

4. **Non-Repudiation**

What would happen if Bob received a message from Alice but she says she never sent it? Digital signatures are one way that cryptography is used to make sure this cannot happen

Different Cryptography Types

Earlier, I told you what the three main types of cryptography were and now I will go into a little more detail on each one.

1. **SKC – Secret Key Cryptography – Symmetric Encryption**

With the secret key method of encryption, just one key is used for the encryption and the decryption. A sender will encrypt a plaintext message using the key and turn it into ciphertext. This is then sent to the recipient and the same key will then decrypt the message back into plaintext so it can be read. The key must be known by both parties and is the secret to this form of encryption.

SKC schemes are usually known as stream or block ciphers. A stream cipher works on one byte at a time and puts a mechanism in place for feedback so the key changes constantly. Two of the more common stream ciphers are:

- **Self-Synchronizing** – These ciphers will calculate every bit in a key string. They are calculated as functions of the previous n-bit and are called as such because the decryption process stays synchronous with the encryption process by knowing how far it is into the n-bit keystream.

- **Synchronous** – these stream ciphers will generate a key stream that is independent of the message stream, but through the use of the same keystream generation with both the sender and the recipient.

Block ciphers encrypt data a block at a time and use the same key with each block. The difference between the two ciphers is that, with a block cipher, the plaintext message always encrypts to an identical ciphertext when the same key is used whereas, with the stream cipher, the plaintext encrypts to a different ciphertext each time.

2. **PKC – Public Key Cryptography – Asymmetric Cryptography**

It is claimed that PKC is the most significant of all cryptographic developments in the last 400 years. This kind of cryptography depends on one-way functions. These are mathematical functions that compute easily as opposed to the inverse function which is more difficult. Look at these examples:

- **Multiplication and Factorization -** Let's say you have a pair of prime numbers, 3 and 7, and you want to calculate the product of those numbers. This should be simple; the product is 21. Now let's suppose that you have a number which is the product of two prime numbers, 21 and you need to work out what the prime factors are. Eventually, you will work them out but it will take you a quite some time to factor than to multiply.

- **Exponentiation and Logarithms –** Let's say that you have the number 3 and you take it to the 6th power. Once again, this is relatively easy to work out – 3 to the power of 6 is 729. But what if you started with 729 and needed to work out what the x and y integers were so that log x 729 were equal to y. This will take much longer to calculate.

These may be reasonably trivial examples but they are representative of the functional pairs that PKC uses – the ease of exponentiation and multiplication and the more difficult tasks of calculating logarithms and factoring. The real "trick" to PKC is in finding the hidden door in a one-way function so that, when we know some information, the inverse calculation is easier.

PKC generally uses two related keys. However, although they are related, knowing what one key is doesn't automatically mean that you can work out what the other is. One encrypts the plaintext and the other key decrypts the ciphertext. What is important is that it makes no difference which order the keys are applied in, just that both are required. This is where the moniker 'asymmetric encryption' comes in.

One of the keys is a public key and whoever owns it can advertise it as much as they want. The other is a private key and is never told or revealed to anyone else. Sending messages using PKC is easy. Alice uses Bob's public key to encrypt a message and Bob will use his private key to decrypt it. Doing it this way, authentication and non-repudiation come into play.

3. Hash Functions

Hash functions are also known as one-way encryption or message digests. They are algorithms that do not use any key; instead, a hash value of fixed length is generated based on the plaintext. This means it is not possible for the length or the content of the plaintext message to be recovered. A hash function provides a digital fingerprint of the contents of a file and this is used to make sure that the file is not tampered with or altered in any way. These are used by operating systems for password encryption.

That is cryptography in a nutshell, the basics of encryption and encryption and the system used by the blockchain to ensure the integrity of every single transaction.

Chapter 2: Autonomy

The definition of autonomy is "freedom from external control or influence" and that defines the essence of blockchain. Nobody owns the blockchain; there is no central regulating or governing body, nobody to 'interfere' in the way it runs. The blockchain is completely independent, unlike the physical cash in your pocket which is owned by the bank, which is printed by the bank for as long as the government gives them permission to print it.

If that's the case, how does the blockchain work? How can it work so smoothly, be so secure when nobody governs it? The answer to that lies in the self-regulation mechanism within the blockchain and that mechanism is called distributed consensus.

What is Distributed Consensus?

It is a term that you will see often in conjunction with the blockchain and with cryptocurrency and it is claimed that solving distributed consensus is the innovation behind Bitcoin and enabled the explosion of alternative currencies or 'alt coins' as they are known. Consensus refers to a process of collective decision-making or where two or more people come to an agreement over what may be true or false. The term is used here in the same way as you would use it in your daily life. One group can come to a decision or a consensus without the need for every person in the group to be unanimously in support.

When a group of electronic devices or computers need to agree with one another about something so that they can operate, there is one central unit who will make the decision and then let the rest of the network know. However, what distributed consensus means is that the computers that make up the network, called nodes, all agree in a way that is more like a group of humans coming to an agreement and that means that each member of the group will come to one collective decision. Similar to how we have a jury in court that collaboratively work together on a verdict if a suspect is guilty or innocent.

What is difficult to grasp is how the network nodes from that distributed consensus operate, and that is even harder to do when one of the nodes is deliberately attempting to manipulate all the others or is lying.

Blockhain is here to stay and establishes a transparent system and methodology of engaging in business transactions that cannot be altered and can be easily accessed by the general public for authentication purposes. By implementing this sort of technology we eliminate the many pitfalls we are faced with today in regards to fraud, embezzlement and other financial infringements.

This innovative technology eliminates the need of centralized and authoritative systems to dictate and regulate society. The future is here and now we can rely on a decentralized system to level out the playing field in the world we live in today. Think about it?

Blockchain technology uses what is called a hyper ledger which essentially records all transactions that occurs and is stored on the blockchain system. Imagine your bank statements, but in a more expansive and larger scope, every single little detail from small purchases to large is recorded. Worldwide access to the public means there will no longer be a need for a central system to regulate financial transactions, ie: Financial institutions, banks, etc.

We live in the digital age and it would only make sense that currency would eventually follow in the transition into the digital realm, ie: cryptocurrency. This is not merely speculation or abstract conjecture, but this is based on trends and a few facts. Let's take a look at some of the things we interface with on a daily basis that have also stepped into the world digitization.

Books - In the past libraries were the only source to get access to books and other information packages. But, now we have digital books (kindle, Kobo,etc).

Music/Podcasts - Before you had to buy records, tapes, and CDs to listen to your favorite artist. Now we have itunes and other platforms that allow you to instantly listen to music without having to go through the hassle of buying an actual physical product. Digital access to music eliminates the damaged merchandise factor, for example a scratch on a CD would render the music on it inaudible, meaning you would have to go buy another copy! With music being digital you eliminate such inconveniences.

Video Games - Synonymous to music this too has stepped into the digital era. Games use to be purchased on cartridges and most recently CDs, but now can all be downloaded at the touch of a button online for instant access.

Mail - Before the invention of the E-mail the vast majority of people in society solely relied on mail couriers (mail men/women) as a means of relaying communication. However, since the advent and successful launch of the E-mail people now communicate worldwide with lightning speed! Uninterrupted by time zones and other external factors.

Bill Payments -   In the past the average person had to rely on cheques to get paid and to exchange large volumes of cash in any given transaction. Bills would have to be paid by cheque, and the period of waiting times were immensely long.   But, now we have direct deposits (Electronic Wire Transfers) and other similar electronic deposits. We can even make bill payments and purchases directly from our smart   phones!

Not only that but we can even deposit cheques via apps through our phones electronically! (most big banks have this feature)   Physical stores are starting to dwindle in size and their profit margins are greatly diminishing due to "online customers" , simply because in this day in age people value convenience and instant gratification above all things. Buying online saves you the hassle of traveling to the store, attempting to find parking, and the heartache of finding out the product you were looking for is out of stock.

The list goes on and on, but I would imagine you get the point by now, and can see a trend of digitization rapidly growing and shows no signs of slowing down. So take these examples as evidence of a potential shift and boom in cryptocurrency! Blockchain is the technology behind bitcoin and various other cryptocurrencies and the trend to adopt blockchain is inevitable.

There are a plethora of multimillion dollar companies investing into blockchain technology for good reason, as it is now being seen as the new building block of the foreseeable future.

When it comes to money people have to place their trust into a third party to facilitate a transaction. Blockchain utilizes complex algorithms, math and cryptography and a transparent open centralized data base. Thus, creating a record that can be authenticated by the general public. The potential for blockchain is boundless, and almost anyone with an internet connection would be able to utilize this technology.

The far reaching prowess and implications are endless, perhaps in the near future it will be used to efficiently collect taxes, help immigrants send money back home who don't have access to financial institutions, and much, much more!

Blockchain will be met with some opposition from governments, financial and legal institutions due to the nature of its autonomy. With any new advancements we must embrace it and hold it to the utmost accountability, the revolution of blockchain technology is here and it is up to us to enable it.

At any period of time in civilization it's a known fact any new ideas, notions, knowledge and even technology has been blasted with extreme scrutiny, will blockchain undergo the same? It's hard to say and give a conclusive answer to this question, but what I can say is people and huge corporations are investing in blockchain by the droves as the potential is there.

We all want a system that is transparent, where records could be stored, facts authenticated, and ultimately security is guaranteed. Blockchain technology enables us to have all these incredible features, storing information on a network of computers and distributing information. Meaning no one person has ownership over the system!

The people who utilize blockchain submit bundles of information/records known as "blocks" in a chronological irreversible chain (hence the name blockchain). Now I'd like to briefly discuss some highlights of the hyper ledger used within blockchain technology, we will discuss this more in depth further in the book.

Distributed

Since this ledger is distributed it works as an open data base which shares all records stored in the blockchain. Accessible to anyone around the world who has access to an internet connection, and no one person is privy to this information. When an item is purchased through blockchain it goes through a series of authentication processes by involving everyone who must give consent to the occurring transaction, and they will all posses every record, history and piece of data on the purchased item.

Authenticated

No transaction can be altered or added to the blockchain without being recorded permanently and would need the consent of all parties involved to verify it. This eliminates the risk any fraudulent activities.

Secure

How trustworthy is blockchain? Certificates of authenticity, real time records, and product details are all available to secure and authenticate any existing transaction. At the end of a transaction there is a auditable and transparent record of information that validates authenticity. It doesn't matter whether its gold, diamonds, food, contracts deeds, etc. Blockchain technology will transform the world, it speeds up processes, increases cash flow, lowers transaction costs, and ultimately establishes trust among users.

Practical Example

Gold a commodity that has held immense value since the beginning of human civilization. In regards to commerce the framework of complex intermediaries involved surrounding gold can be quite overwhelming and time consuming, ranging from legal, regulatory, quality assurance, financial, and manufacturing bodies.

You have to run through a labyrinth consisting of government officials, lawyers, accountants, banks, sellers and middlemen. This is the current standard in which we operate in today and is an insecure methodology of practice to say the least. Smuggled gold or unethically derived gold can arise and be sold under the radar without any assurance.

However, blockchain technology will change all of that with what is known as a "hyper ledger". This will synchronize all transactions that occur and record each sequence from beginning to end. This technology enables us to trace the point of origin of gold from the mines right to the hands of consumers with pinpoint accuracy, transparency and reliability.

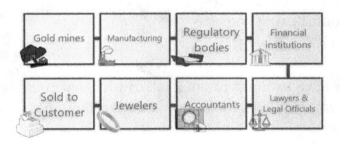

Blockchain technology, explained through gold.

Bitcoin Distributed Consensus

The birth of Bitcoin came about from the thought that a network of digital currency could operate in a true P2P (peer to peer) manner, without any interference from any central authority. The potential here is that we can now reduce the reliance that we have on banks that claim to be too big to fail, banks who create and control new money for their own interests. That control would be placed squarely back in the hands of the people where it belongs.

In order for P2P money to work as it should, every network member needs to agree on the number of coins that all the other members own in order to prevent something called double-spending and to prevent fraud and theft.

Bitcoin, and by relation the blockchain, uses the process of "mining" to solve this distributed consensus problem. Any network member can decide to mine, but there is no requirement for you to become a miner in order to get some use out of the Bitcoin network. The miners are given rewards in the form of new Bitcoins and in 'older' Bitcoins that is paid by way of transaction fees from other network members.

The mining process uses 'Proof of Work' methodology to make sure that the consensus is correct and true. As well, it relies on game theory mechanics; this means that the design ensures that cheating and dishonesty is not in the best interests of any participant, even an incredibly selfish one. Let me try to put this in as simple a way as I can – each miner will perform an inordinate number of calculations. Each of these calculations will give the miner the opportunity to mine a transaction block, which contains all transactions that have taken place in a set time period and they can keep the reward that comes out of that block. However, for the network to accept the block, all the other miners on the network must confirm it or agree with the transaction history version on the network. The majority of that network will form the distributed consensus and this is done through the Proof of Work calculations and not the individuals.

If someone were to attempt to lie, the other miners would need to call them on it. Because each miner must maintain theory version of the history, it wouldn't be in their best interests to allow the lie to go through. This means that a malicious user could only manipulate the consensus to accept the fake transaction history by doing more proof of work calculations than all the rest of the network put together.

If a network member is not in agreement with the consensus, they will then 'fork' that network, creating another transaction branch history which will be different from the others. This will not be accepted by any user as a true part of the blockchain.

This means that the blockchain for Bitcoin depends on the hash-rate – this is how many calculations are performed by the network. They are called hashes simply because the mathematical name is 'secure hash algorithm'. If there are not many proof of work calculations being done, the entire network is considered insecure – any attacker would need to spend little to gain more than 50% of the hashing power and could then carry out a 51% attack. If large numbers are being performed, it could cost a lot more to buy the necessary computing power to do this. Because of the size of the network today, it would cost so much to carry out this attack that it simply wouldn't be practical nor profitable to do so.

Although I have talked mainly in terms of Bitcoin, simply because it was the first use, the above explains the self-regulating mechanism of any blockchain. It matters not what it is used for, only that it will work to secure the network no matter what.

Chapter 3: Practical Uses

The blockchain, as you now know, is the underlying technology for Bitcoin and other cryptocurrencies but, while these may be the headline-grabbers, the blockchain technology has moved further on and is now being adopted quite rapidly across a diverse selection of industries.

Because the blockchain is decentralized and because it is tamper-proof, it is the ideal technology for all different sectors and one area that it has been enjoying enormous success is in smart contracts. A smart contract is a piece of code that will run when conditions that are specifically defined are met. The uses of a smart contract are virtually limitless, especially where the result required is exchange. Many companies are now using these smart contracts in the supply chain to ensure the quality of their products and the dispatch of them.

What other industries could possibly adopt the blockchain technology though? Believe it or not, there are several practical uses for the blockchain and here are the five most exciting ones.

The Finance Sector

All the blockchain headlines have centered on cryptocurrency but in the meantime, the mainstream finance sector has been studying the blockchain technology for years and, now you know how it works, it's clear why they have been doing this. By using blockchain technology in their applications, they can significantly reduce the amount of time it takes for many internal processes and this will achieve three main things – a cut in costs and time, the elimination of third-party transaction recording and an increase in trust and security.

The Retail Sector

The retail sector is another that has long been researching this technology and its uses in the sector is increasing every day. By far the most valuable application for blockchain is in the guarantee of product, especially the high-value products like art and diamonds. Retailers are also in the forefront in their use of the blockchain to protect their customers from fraud. The potential for this technology is endless product tracking, item identification, location, time tracking, document management etc,. This functions similar to a QR code in regards to authentication and cannot be cheated.

The Agriculture Sector

Both farmers and the consumers are using blockchain technology to track a product from the first stage of rearing or growing right through to the end-purchase. It gives farmers the opportunity to ask for higher prices because they can guarantee their products are of quality and the consumers can see where their product has originated from with pinpoint accuracy.

The Insurance Sector

This is new era for blockchain technology, and is an exciting one too simply because the insurance industry spends, on average, around

$2 billion every year on compliance and fraud prevention. Blockchain technology could make this process simpler by giving the insurance companies better access to data that is more reliable and by providing a link between the provider and the customer

The Energy Sector

Energy companies can use blockchain technology to provide consumers with complete transparency, allowing them to see exactly where their energy is supplied from, how it gets generated and how it is distributed. Consumers will also be able to make use of applications that are based on blockchain technology to gain accurate data about their use of energy, which will give them the ability to make more informed decisions and save money.

Business Case Studies

Blockchain technology safety lies in it being a distributed technology and not a centralized network. For the hacker, this means that getting access to sources of data means needing to hack into every single computer or node on the distributed network simultaneously – not the easiest of hacks! - Virtually impossible. The computing power that would be required for this kind of hack has previously been compared to being equivalent to the "hashing power of a nation state" along with all the tech companies in that nation state.

There are those that say the blockchain cannot be considered as a disruptive technology but is, instead, a foundational technology as it provides a structure and underlying framework for transactions in the future that involves anything of value. Let's have a look at some case studies and how blockchain technology could be put to use.

Case Study 1 – Banking

Our current banking systems are extremely vulnerable to fraud and recent example is Brazil. A group of hackers took over control of all the ATM and online operations of one of the largest Brazilian banks for several hours. In this time, they gained access to credit card information, passwords and a lot of other so-called secure information and anyone who logged in during that time was not aware they were being routed to a fake copy of the bank's site.

Middlemen like banks are not necessary with blockchain technology. The valuable information would not have been stored in a central access point, the bank website in this case, and it certainly wouldn't have been possible for the hackers to get access to all that information in those few hours.

Case Study 2 – Government Fraud and Corruption

US government officials were carrying out an investigation into extortion, theft and many other crimes on "Silk Road" on the internet. For those that don't know, the online Silk Road was an online darknet black market, originally used for drug selling and money laundering. The blockchain ledger that was in use turned up a very interesting fact – two of the FBI agents that were on the task force were, in fact, behind the criminal activity. The pair had tried to cover their tracks but, because blockchain is a publicly accessible ledger, that cannot be altered, and because it is decentralized, they couldn't hide from the truth or cover their tracks. The power of the blockchain lies in its ability to be completely transparent – nothing can be hidden from anyone.

The Pros and Cons of the Blockchain Technology

Everything has a good side and everything has a bad side and blockchain technology is no different. Here we look at the basic pros and cons of the technology:

Pros

- Anything that is of value may be transferred confidentially and safely, without risk of alteration
- All transactions are verified on a P2P network
- In times of economic crises, cryptocurrencies cannot be frozen like cash in your bank
- There will be no need for third-parties, like banks, government, lawyers, etc.
- No transaction can be reversed

Cons

- Scammers can use the anonymity of the technology for their own malicious use

- Manipulation and hacking is still possible, albeit on a small scale
- Most offices, governments, retailers, and others that deal with money have no real understanding of cryptocurrencies, let alone accept them as currency
- There is likely to be a great deal of resistance due to many people being employed in the middlemen jobs
- Transactions cannot be reversed

Going back to one of the downsides, because there are so many people employed by the banks, governments and other middlemen institutions, acceptance of blockchain technology won't be easy. However, these institutions are highly vulnerable to fraud, human error and corruption and this really does leave the door wide open for a better, safer way of carrying out transactions. At the end of the day, it is because there is so much fraud and corruption, not to mention the errors and the costs to the consumer that blockchain technology was created.

Be it banking, insurance, or any other industry, one thing is sure – we are going to see a lot of change in the future as these industries begin to adopt blockchain technology and, although it is expected to take many years for full adoption, businesses of today need to start planning now if they want to be on the cutting edge.

Risks of the Blockchain

Although blockchain technology offers a great deal of promise, adoption of it requires some very sound risk management to be put in place and that will require a full understanding of all the risks attached. Right now, the obvious risk revolves around Bitcoin and other cryptocurrencies on the blockchain, but as things evolve and new applications arise, those risks will change.

Take legacy insurance policies, for example. These might not have protection in place for a company that maintains bitcoin or any other blockchain asset and some may exclude anything to do with Bitcoin. Others might exclude digital currency or electronic data which means if your Bitcoin is lost, tough. You won't be able to claim on insurance for them!

There are other risks at consideration here – given that the value of Bitcoin fluctuates in fiat currency, how will their value be determined? And insurance isn't the only consideration; we also must consider regulatory risk management. This is somewhat complicated because new regulations are written, but the old ones will still be in effect and not all countries have the same rules. Some areas of focus for the legitimate business that wants the benefit of the technology while staying firmly above board include:

- AML – Anti- Money Laundering
- KYC – Know Your Customer
- Obligations in tax and accounting

One recent example of how regulators are applying the existing laws to new technologies is a subpoena from the IRS to CoinBase, one of the largest cryptocurrency exchanges in the world.

While Blockchain may have its benefits, the further into the mainstream it goes, the more important risk management will be.

Chapter 4: Blockchain Security Measures

The blockchain is a structure that allows for a digital transactions ledger to be produced and shared over a digital network. The distributed ledger technology is going to enable capital markets and the financial services industry to unlock their full potential in terms of the digital markets by helping them to move on from the inefficient and expensive systems in use today. But just how secure is the blockchain?

It is, in fact, one of the most secure technologies ever created, promising to remove the risks of tampering, cyber crime and fraud and all of this is down to the math beneath the chain, the math that swaddles each transaction in a layer of protection. Distributed ledgers can increase trust because every party in the transaction receives a copy of it. The transaction participants cannot make any changes to the transaction registry; all they can do is add to it and the original transaction is intact and in irreversible. In traditional models, hackers only need to access a database and change a single value to divert the funds; with the blockchain, this cannot be done.

The Chain of Trust

Another one of the major promises of the blockchain exchanges is to establish provenance. Distributed records will establish a complete history of everything in a supply chain. If an issue is found with a specific part, perhaps a dodgy brake pad, the car manufacturers would be able to quickly locate the supplier, the date of manufacture and the production line. This all makes it much easier to narrow down the likelihood of recalls. On top of that, unscrupulous suppliers wouldn't be able to hide anything because they cannot make any changes to that database.

Cyber Security at its Best

The blockchain provides us with an alternative ways of storing data and sharing information, that takes away the single failure points and centralization of traditional methods that can easily be hacked. The technology behind Bitcoin can now be used as a way of beefing up security and preventing cybercrime and it can do this in three ways:

1. **Identity Protection**

One of the commonest forms of encryption used to secure messages, emails, websites and any other communication form online is PKI – Public Key Infrastructure. However, most of the time PKI implementations require trusted, centralized third-party certificate authorities to issue the key pairs, revoke them or store them for every single participant and that gives hackers chance to use them for spoofing identities and cracking encryptions. A recent example is WhatsApp, one of the most popular messaging apps in the world! – it was shown it could be exploited to generate false keys and allow *MITM* **(man-in-the-middle)** attacks. These are attacks when hackers secretly alter communication with two recipients, but the two parties are not privy to this and believe they have a secured line, but in actual fact it's tampered.

By publishing keys on the blockchain, this risk is eliminated and applications will easily be able to verify the identity of whom you are communicating with. Pomcor, a tech research company, recently published a blueprint for a blockchain that is based on PKI but does not eliminate central authorities. Instead, the blockchain is used for storing hashes of certificates that have been issued or revoked. In this way, users can verify certificate authenticity through a transparent and decentralized source.

2. **Data Integrity**

We use private keys for signing files and documents so that the recipient can verify the data source. Then we go to extraordinary lengths to prove that no tampering has taken place and this is where the problem lies – that key is meant to be private! There is, however, a blockchain alternative and it replaces the private with transparency, distributes the evidence over all the nodes on the network and makes it impossible to manipulate any data without being caught out.

KSI, or Keyless Signature Structure, is a new blockchain project that has one aim – to get rid of key-based authentication. It stores hashes of files and data on the blockchain and verifies copies of that data through hashing algorithms; the results are compared with the original on the blockchain and if anything has been changed, it will swiftly be caught.

The military is already considering KSI for the protection of sensitive data while health care providers are using the blockchain for change-auditing, transparency of data and access-control for health records. This is incredibly important given the amount of sensitive data that is handled by the healthcare providers and the number of times they have been victims of data breaches. The blockchain technology can help them to verify patient data integrity across organizations, create audit trails that cannot be changed and maintain the integrity of clinical trial data.

3. Critical Infrastructure Protection

In October, a major DDOS (Distributed Denial of Service) attack taught every one of us how easily hackers can bring critical services to their knees. One single service that provided the DNS for most of the major websites was brought down, cutting off access to Netflix, Twitter, PayPal and many other services for hours. This is just one more example of how centralized infrastructures fail us.

Using the blockchain to store the DNS entries would significantly improve security because it eliminates the one target that a hacker can use to bring the system down. One of the biggest weak points in the current system is caching, which makes it easy for a hacker to stage a DDOS attack against the servers and allows censorship of social media and manipulation of DNS registries by oppressive regimes. None of that will be possible on the blockchain because caching does not exist and because the entire chain is transparent.

A DNS that is distributed and transparent will give owners control of their own records and will stop any person or agency from manipulating the entries as they want to.

The Hyperledger Project

We can't talk about the blockchain without talking about Bitcoin, the poster child for the technology. Bitcoin has been widely shunned by financial institutions because it started life associated with the dark web, because of its lack of accountability and because of its use in ransomware. According to Barclays bank, these financial institutions have a requirement to put measures in place to know their customers and to stop money laundering.

This is why the Hyperledger Project was developed. It is an open-source project that has the support of banks, large manufacturers and insurance companies to address those very real concerns. Features of the Hyperledger include trust insurance, transparency and the ability to use smart contracts. Some of the biggest supporters of the Hyperledger are American Express, London Stock Exchange, JP Morgan Chase & Co and Wells Fargo and one of the tools that has come out of this is something called the Hyperledger Fabric.

Hyperledger was founded in 2015 by the Linux Foundation to advance blockchain technology across industries. Instead of using a single blockchain standard, the project encourages the development of blockchain technologies using a collaborative approach, through a community process and a series of intellectual property rights that will encourage key standard adoption and open development.

Fabric is one of the projects and, like the blockchain, it has the ledger, it makes use of smart contracts and is a system that participants can manage their own transactions in. Where Fabric differs from other blockchains is that it is a private and a permissioned system. Instead of requiring 'proof of work', Fabric members enroll in the network using a membership services provider.

Fabric offers its members:

- The ability to store ledger data in multiple formats
- Consensus mechanisms that may be switched in and out
- Channel creation – groups of participants can create their own separate transactions ledger. This is important where some network

participants may not want their competitors to see every transaction they make

Shared Ledgers

The Fabric Ledger subsystem is made up of two components – transaction log and world state. Each of the participants will have a copy of the ledger for each Fabric network they are a member of. World State describes the ledger at any given point and is the ledger database while the transaction log will record every transaction that has resulted in that World State – basically, it is an update history.

Smart Contracts

Smart contracts for Fabric are written using chaincode and these are invoked by blockchain-external applications when there is a need for the application and the ledger to interact. Most of the time, chaincode will only have an interaction with the World State and not the transaction log.

Privacy

Depending on the network requirements, B2B (Business to Business) network participants may well be sensitive about the information that is being shared while for other types of network this may not be such a big concern. Hyperledger Fabric supports those networks that require privacy as an operational requirement as well as those that are open.

Consensus

All transactions must be written to the ledger in the exact order that they happen, although they may not be between the same participants on that network. For this, the transaction order must be established and a method putting in place for rejecting those bad transactions that have been put on the ledger, either in error or for malicious purposes.

Hyper Ledger Fabric was designed to give network starters the option of choosing the best consensus mechanism to suit their needs, retaining privacy, trust, and transparency while being flexible enough to suit all industry types.

Hash Functions & Ledger

What about our names being publically broadcasted on the ledger for public view? No worries, this is solved by something we earlier discussed called a "hash function" which disguises people's identity with a 20 digit unique code (mathematical equation). Masking their real identities and details in a complex arrangement of numbers.

How do we know we are starting from the same transaction version of the record? This can be also addressed by a hash function as well, codes will be compared from computer to computer and if the codes all match it will be verified as accurate. Remember hackers would need to tamper with ledgers from every single computer involved in the transaction to alter information, which is highly unlikely. Making this technology and information of the ledger reliable.

Chapter 5: Bitcoin

Bitcoin is the best and most well-known use of the blockchain and, although blockchain technology is moving onto bigger and better things, Bitcoin will always be the first thing we think of. Bitcoin was the very first and, so far, most successful digital currency. They are created through the act of 'mining' and this involves the use of very expensive hardware to solve mathematical equations. Each 'miner' is rewarded with a Bitcoin or a part of one. The most basic explanation of the Bitcoin is that it is electricity that has been converted into strings of code, each of which has a monetary value.

Why is Bitcoin Controversial?

There are several reasons for this, not least the fact that Bitcoin was used for illegal activities online. From 2011 to 2013, criminal traders purchased batches of Bitcoin costing millions of dollars, purely to get it under the radar and this forced the price of the Bitcoin up. Truthfully though, the real reason why the Bitcoin is so controversial is because it is decentralized; there is no middleman and the power has been taken from the federal banks and given back to the people – and the banks don't like that. Unlike the bank account you hold now, a Bitcoin account cannot be frozen, terminated and it cannot be looked into by the tax man. We also don't need a bank or any other agency to govern Bitcoin – we can do it ourselves.

Although the Bitcoin is a digital or cryptocurrency, as soon as you own them they start to act as physical currency – they have a value and can be traded or used exactly as physical currency. You can buy services or goods with them or you can store them in a digital wallet and hope that the value goes up in time. The wallet is a requirement for buying, using and selling Bitcoin; it is a database, online or offline, that is stored on your computer or another device, or even in the cloud and this is where your coins are kept.

Regulations and Values

The value of a Bitcoin can change daily; sometimes up, sometimes down. Right now, more than millions of Bitcoin are in circulation and the mining continues to dredge up more. However, when the number of Bitcoin in existence reaches 21 million, around about the year 2040, they will stop being created. The Bitcoin is divisible so, when you are purchasing or selling you can do so in bits of a Bitcoin if you wish. The current denominations are:

- Bitcoin = 1,000,000 Bits = 100,000,000 Satoshi
- Bits = 0.0000001 (one-millionth) Bitcoin
- Satoshi = 0.00000001 (one-hundred-millionth) Bitcoin

Bitcoin is not regulated in any way, shape or form. It is a self-contained currency and there is no collateral, like a precious metal, behind it.

How the Bitcoin is Made

A Bitcoin is a data ledger file and is called a blockchain. The blockchain is made up of three components:

- The identifying address – an address generated by your wallet and required for all transactions
- A history – the ledger, showing the history of the coin
- The private key header log – where a digital signature is stored confirming all transactions for the file. These signatures are unique to the user and their wallet.

It is these keys that are the backbone of the Bitcoin security. Each trade is tracked, it is tagged and then it is disclosed publicly. The signatures are confirmed across the network of miners which stops duplicated transactions and forgeries.

An interesting fact worth noting at this point is that, although the digital address of every wallet a Bitcoin touches is recorded, no personal details are, such as name, address or any other identifying detail and this is what makes the system anonymous. And, although your Bitcoin is stored on your device, the history of them is on a public ledger, providing transparency, and deterring the use of Bitcoin for illegal purposes.

Fees

There are no bank fees to pay because no banks are involved. There is, however, a small fee for using Bitcoin. The fees are split between the servers who support the miners, the exchanges that convert the Bitcoin to fiat currency and the mining pools that you may be involved in. These fees are minuscule compared to conventional banking or transfer fees.

Practical Use Cases

1. **Donations** - to non-government approved causes, such as Wikileaks
2. **Purchases** - of goods that the government doesn't approve of. In 2011 for example, the New York State Senator publicly demonstrated how cryptocurrencies were being used to purchase drugs online for home delivery. This resulted in a huge Bitcoin price bubble
3. **Gambling** – there are a lot of online gambling sites that allow users to deposit funds and claim winnings in Bitcoin. The winnings area paid to the

same Bitcoin address that deposited the funds, cutting out banks and any other financial agency from the equation.

4. **Purchasing Services** – again, that the government doesn't approve of. A recent example is an Escort site that suddenly found itself unable to make payments for ads through traditional means and turned to Bitcoin. There are also several cam sites that operate only on Bitcoin and other sites that use Bitcoin as a way of gaining privacy and anonymity.

5. **Hiding Assets** – usually in a divorce case and not something you will see much about because of the serious issues it could cause with family. Obviously, this could also be used to hide assets for other reasons, such as bankruptcy and from the government for one reason or another.

6. **Cross-Border Transfers** – Bitcoin is not just used as a way of storing and hiding wealth. One of the most powerful aspects of the blockchain will come when the larger economies rise and/or fall. This is historic and will always happen and this is why there are so many global reserve currencies in the world. Traditionally, gold reserves were

used to transfer value but this is not so useful in the digital world. Bitcoin will be the next method of transferring this value across borders.

These are more extreme and out of the way cases, but together with the traditional purchases that you can make with Bitcoin, they all point towards the sheer power that an unregulated, decentralized digital currency can have.

Chapter 6: How the Blockchain is Changing the World

Just lately, blockchain technology has attracted a great deal of attention. As one of the most innovative way of creating contracts and organizing transactions, the blockchain has a real potential to change how we deal with money. The blockchain has been the underlying technology for Bitcoin cryptocurrency since 2008 and there is a good reason why it is such an important technology – it is the only way for secure transactions to be made without interference from a third-party. It is this that makes it a useful technology, not just for cash but for other social organization forms, like voting, work or property.

The name blockchain comes about because each transaction is added to a time-stamped block, each transaction having its own history and each block containing a hash function or key to the next block, thus joining it together.

This blockchain technology is representing nothing less than a regeneration of the internet and it has the potential to transform everything, from money to business, from governments to society.

Think about this – when you send something over the internet to another person, be it an email, a PDF or .DOC file, or a JPG you are not sending them the original, merely a copy. Depending on what rights the recipients have, they might be able to print the copy but you cannot print money. For that, we must put our trust in a series of powerful middlemen like banks, and governments. These banks and governments, even social media sites to a certain extent, work hard to establish who we are and our asset ownership. In short, they assist us in settling transactions and transferring value.

They don't do a bad job but they do have their limitations. They make use of central servers – these can be hacked into. They charge fees for what they do, sometimes high fees like 10% of the value of a transfer to another country for example. They hold on to our data, undermining what privacy we have. They are not always reliable and most certainly are not always fast at what they do. They also cut out more than 2 billion people who have insufficient means to open a bank account.

This is where the blockchain steps in and takes over, the first ever digital medium for full P2P value exchange, Distributed computations and a real heavy-duty encryption system ensure the integrity of all the data that is traded over millions of different devices without ever going through any third-party. The trust has been hard-coded into the blockchain platform and therefore it is called the Trust Protocol. The blockchain is an accounts ledger, it is a database, a sentry, a notary and it is a clearinghouse, all rolled into one and all by consensus.

But why would you care about this? What difference will it mean to you? Perhaps you love music and you want artists to be able to earn a living from their music. Perhaps you are an aid worker and to rebuild homes after a natural disaster you need to be able to identify homeowners. Maybe you are a public citizen who has had enough of politicians not being transparent or accountable. It doesn't really matter what you are or who you are; someone, somewhere is, right now, building applications based on blockchain technology that will serve your purpose and these are only the tip of the iceberg.

Every single business, every government, agency, and individual can get some benefit from the blockchain. Let's face it, it is already causing severe disruption to the financial services industry. The internet of things, all those devices connected, sending and receiving data, generating their own power, trading it, the ones that protect the environment, help us to manage our health and our homes – this internet of things will eventually require a ledger of everything!

Social inequality is on the rise the poor keep getting poorer and the rich keep exponentially increasing their wealth. The gap continuously grows between the two and, by using the blockchain we can change; no longer will we distribute wealth, we will distribute opportunity and value on a fair basis. Yes, there will be winners and there will be losers, but, so long as we do this right, the blockchain can be the beginning of a new era and age of prosperity for everyone.

4 Unexpected Ways the Blockchain Could Change the World

1. Distributed Cloud Storage

Already, the blockchain has undergone some change to improve security measures so that information can be stored in a way that is unscaleable. As well as being something of a techie hobby, the storage of data on the blockchain could also be seen as disruptive. Right now, cloud storage services are all centralized, meaning a user places their trust into one provider. The blockchain will decentralize this. Take Stori for example, which is a cloud storage facility currently in beta. It uses a network powered by the blockchain to improve security and reduce dependency. Users can rent out any extra storage capacity they have, enabling the traditional cloud to be stored more than 300 times over. Cloud storage currently costs the world $22 billion a year and the ability to rent excess space will do two things – provide a revenue stream for some users and cut the cost of cloud data storage to personal and business users.

2. **Contracts That Cannot Be Broken**

A smart contract is one that is self-executing or self-enforcing. The role that the blockchain plays in these contracts is to take the place of the third-party that is normally needed to resolve legal disputes. Tokens, otherwise known as 'colored coins' or 'smart properties' may be used as representatives of asset and the ability to hard-code the ownership transfer when you trade the assets can create what we call 'unbreakable' contracts.

Take a widget factory, for example. They currently produce red widgets only, but they get an order from a brand-new customer, for 100 blue widgets. The factory now has to purchase new machinery to service this order and the only way they could possibly get their investment back is for the customer to go through with the order.

In the traditional world, the factory would trust the customer to pay or they would hire a lawyer to enforce the contract – this costs mega-bucks.

With the blockchain, they can create a smart property that has a self-executing contract – this contract could say that for every widget delivered, a specific price per item is taken from the customer's bank account and out in the factory account. This does two things – cuts out the need for a deposit or the use of an escrow account, which uses a third-party, and it protects the customer by stopping the factory from not delivering or under delivering.

Right now, this is mostly just theory but already Ethereum platform is pulling the smart contract closer to being a reality.

3. No More Patents

In the same way as the Smart Contract platforms, (PoE) ProofOfExistence.com has already launched a series of basic legal services that can be used. This is one of the first recorded uses of the blockchain that is not financial in nature. PoE will store information that is encrypted on the blockchain, recording a transaction hash which cannot be replaced and is associated with a document that is not stored on the blockchain.

The obvious case for this is patents. Let's say Samsung or Apple wanted to prove that they created a specific technology on a specific date but they don't want to file for a public patent. Using the blockchain, the company could prove that ownership by revealing documents that are linked to a specific hash which will show on a specific date on the blockchain.

4. **Electronic Voting**

The current method of having to count every paper and postal vote for an election is becoming archaic, costly in terms of time, money and on accuracy. It is a method that is full of technical issues, such as the accuracy of a machine during a recount cannot be verified and those machines are also huge targets for hackers. In some countries, the blockchain is now being used by political parties for internal voting.

Each transaction on a blockchain contains a hash that verifies the succeeding hash and, in terms of voting, this would mean that, if one vote were changed, millions of other would need to be changed before another can be cast.

The blockchain network is protected simply because there is no hacker alive who has sufficient computing power to do this in such a short space of a time.

Also, because of the anonymity factor, each of the votes can be shared publicly without the voter being identified in any way. In this way, every voter can ensure that their vote has been counted and, one day, the blockchain could signal the end of voting and election corruption.

Blockchain technology has got, potentially, millions of different applications and, while most are still in preliminary development stages now, they will eventually make their way into your life, one way or another. In the future, instead of saying, "look it up on Google", the new buzz phrase is likely to be "check it on blockchain."

Prediction: Changing The World In Many Ways

Banks - Blockhain technology will enable almost everyone around the world, even people living in third world countries to have the means of financial access via bitcoin (BTC). - BTC uses fundamental blockchain technology to function.

Cyber Security - Although blockchain is accessible to the public it uses complex math and cryptography to enhance security, thus making it extremely difficult for anyone to hack and tamper with it.

Supply Chain Management - All transactions are permanently recorded in sequential order from point of begging to end, and constantly monitored through general consensus among the blockchain network for accuracy and authenticity purposes.- Increasing efficiency, reducing errors and time delays.

Insurance - Insurance is based on the principal of trust management, blockchain can be used to accurately verify data, such as insured person's identity, residence, etc. The chances for fraud is extremely slim as you know blockchain has state of the art advanced security measures.

Transportation - We've all heard of Uber? Well now blockchain is looking to create decentralized peer to peer ride sharing apps, ways for car owners and users to establish terms and conditions of transportation without third party intermediaries (Uber).

Charity - Common issues with charities are corruption and inefficiencies. Blockchain technology will ensure transparent record keeping and create a permanent sequential, tamper resistant record to track, so there are no chances of money scandals or frauds we always hear about in the news. Ensuring only the intended recipient receives the funds.

Voting - Voting scandals and rigging can happen anywhere in the world, and even here in the west we are not immune to scandals, remember the 2016 US election? It's not the first time political parties have been accused for rigging results. Blockchain technology can be utilized for voter registration and identity confirmation , and also electronic vote counting would ensure only legitimate votes are counted.

No votes could be taken away or added, thus creating an indisputable publically accessible ledger. How's that for democracy?

Governments - Government system are often slow, ambiguous and extremely frustrating. Implementing blockchain based systems will decrease bureaucracy, increase efficiency and uphold transparency.

Health Care - Secure storage platforms for information utilizing blockchain technology will enhance security and prevent hacking. Safely storing data such as medical records and sharing it only with the intended recipient. Improving data security and possibly even speed up diagnosis.

Energy Management - This has been a centralized monopoly for the longest time. But with blockchain technology you would be able to buy forms of energy, ie : electricity in a peer to peer fashion, thus electricity producers and users could buy directly from each other on a decentralized system. Currently we have to use trusted private intermediaries.

Online Music - Blockchain technology is working on a way to pay musicians and artists directly, instead of forfeiting large chunks of royalties to platforms or record labels. Artists/musicians would be able to keep more of the their profits!

Retail - Connecting buyers and sellers without additional fees. Exchanging in commerce without middlemen or intermediaries. In this case blockchain technology would use smart contract systems, and built in reputation management systems.

Real Estate - Eliminate the archaic paper based record keeping system, fraud, and uphold transparency. Blockchain would ensure ownership, accuracy, and even transferring property deeds.

Crowd Funding - A lot of companies use crowd funding platforms, however often times these platforms charge high fees. Blockchain could eliminate these fees by implementing smart contracts and online reputation based systems. New projects would release funds by generating their own "tokens" that have an associated value, and later be exchanged for products, services or cash.

Merkel Tree

In cryptography a "merkel tree" refers to all transactions of a block that are hashed together forming tree like pattern, until a merkel root is reached. (full explanation next page)

Diagram Below:

            ABCD (Merkel Root)

           ^(Branch)

    AB   **CD**

  A ^ B   C ^D

Breakdown: A & B = **AB** , C & D = **CD** , AB & CD = **ABCD**

Merkel Tree Details :

By now you have looked at the merkel tree diagram and are probably wondering what it all means? The merkel tree is considered a data structure I'll elaborate, the bottom 4 values **"A^B" & "C^D"** are hashed together with a branch (^).

Hash = ^

Now imagine each one of these values represents a transaction in a block (A,B,C,D). In order for all the nodes to validate the transactions, this would require a large amount of computation resources and storage. If we had a mobile app that utilized blockchain it wouldn't be realistic to send all these transactions to the app. Thus, we need a way to validate the transaction without sending all of them at once.

So how do we arrive to a solution? Well, we simply hash them together   as previously mentioned:

We hash $A \wedge B$ creating a totally new value *"AB"*. Ergo, $A \wedge B = AB$

The same exact process is followed for *C & D*. We hash $C \wedge D$ together. Therefore, $C \wedge D =$ *"CD"*. Again we create a totally unique and new value.

Lastly we hash **AB** & **CD** together: **AB ^CD = "ABCD"**

ABCD is the" merkel root". As you can see it is the last blockchain in the series of hashes that connect to it.

Now if we are to change any single piece of these values of A,B,C,D, than the entire merkel root value would change as a result. So when one value alters this in turn changes all the other values as well. For example if you were to change the initial values at the bottom of the merkel tree to **A^X** than the **merkel root** would become **"AXCD"**.

Do you see the beauty of the merkel tree? This enables blockchain to be tamper resistant and extremely difficult to cheat. So for example, if a client wanted to validate value "A", what would happen is a computer would use the merkel root "ABCD" and the prior values to validate if in fact value "A" exists on the data structure of the merkel tree.

The merkel root validates the prior sequences in a transaction. Ergo, it is nearly impossible to scam, con or cheat the blockchain system. Usually, you only need the merkel root in order to validate any given value. Since "A" is found in the merkel root it is therefore successfully validated as an accurate value. Let's say, someone tried to change a value, for example purposes lets use "Z". Well than the blockchain system would check the merkel root "ABCD", and since "Z" is not found within this merkel root it is denied and not an accepted value.

Summary

The widespread adoption of blockchain technology is inevitable. When it comes to money people have to place their trust in a third party, whether money, services, goods, etc. However, blockchain technology utilizes math and cryptography providing an open data base that is decentralized, meaning no one has ownership over this system unlike current standards and practices we live with today. Establishing a permanent record that can be verified by the community.

Since the dawn of civilization people have always recorded transactions between the exchange of goods and services on stone tablets and paper. We now have evolved proportionate to the growth of commerce worldwide, and documenting such tasks has become quite complex with various methodologies of documentation, which in a lot of cases gives room for error, fraud and mistakes!

Example

Gold is a precious commodity we used today. This is a prime example of how blockchain technology will enhance security, transparency, efficiency and satisfaction between all parties. Let me elaborate how blockchain will impact this historically treasured rock in a positive manner.

The gold industry has to go through a complex framework consisting of legal, regulatory, financial, manufacturing and other commercial practices. This consists of various intermediaries, lawyers, accountants, banks and legal officials. Current methods posses vulnerabilities and are susceptible to counterfeit gold, corruption and unethically derived gold. As you can see the current arduous process is time consuming and adds to overall cost.

(Gold Mines ---> Manufacturing---> Regulatory bodies --> Financial Institutions --> Lawyers & Legal Officials --> Accountants --->Jewelers --> Sold to Customer.)

Now this is where blockchain comes in and its advanced technology shines, I'll explain, blockchain uses a open source data base, in essence a publicly accessed and authenticated ledger. Blockchain offers all parties involved in the transaction a secure, synchronized and updated sequence of records from point of origins to end. Meaning every single sequence of transaction that occurs is shown on this ledger, ergo creating an irreversible chain of blocks linked together sequentially from beginning to end.

That's why blockchain is favorable and very applicable for implementation in practical everyday use in the world we live in. Imagine being able to find out the origins of an item your purchasing with pinpoint accuracy, transparency and clarity, and not worry about anything unethical surrounding it.

Blockchain: 3 Tamper Resistant Security Features

1.Distributed

Distributed means everyone gets a copy of the ledger meaning there is no "one" centralized system that has ownership of records. -This eliminates any possibilities of tampering with or altering of information. This functions as a shared form of record keeping ensuring no one entity or organization is only privy to it.

2.Authenticated

When an item cycles through the transaction chain, for example gold, everyone not only has access to that information from the ledger, but also authenticates the information through the means of a general consensus among the blockchain network. Information recorded in the blockchain is permanent meaning no one can add to or take away from it, without the consensus of everyone on the network.

3.Secure

Continuing with the example gold, at the end of a transaction cycle certificates of authenticity, real time records, payment transactions, and even product details are provided. As you can see there is a complete auditable and irrefutable record of information accessible to everyone involved in the transaction cycle.

This will make life so much easier for people worldwide. This will eliminate barriers that people have in third world countries and enable their inclusion. This will make sending money back home easier for immigrants where access to financial institutions is limited. Perhaps in the future near blockchain technology will be implemented to collect taxes within countries this way nobody would be able to evade taxes.

The opportunities are boundless and the world is forever changing, what will blockchain technology change next?

Conclusion

Thank you for taking the time to read my book and I truly hope that you now have a much better understanding of the blockchain and what makes it tick. As I said earlier, the blockchain is not simple and it is quite complex. But once you do understand it, you can easily see the benefits of it, not just for you but for the future of finance, for the future of every transaction, be it money, goods or services.

You have seen how Bitcoin works, the single biggest use of the blockchain to date but blockchain technology is leaving Bitcoin behind. It is moving on in leaps and bounds, finding new uses and applications every day, and will eventually become the standard by which we all live by. Centralized agencies, like banks, credit agencies, even governments are fast losing the trust of the people; the fact that they are constantly monitoring every move we make, and always giving us the short end of the stick.

People want to stay anonymous but they want to be safe and secure at the same time. While Bitcoin first started out as a method of money laundering and other criminal activities, it has long moved on and the blockchain is now clean; although many banks and governments still don't trust it because its nefarious start, they are beginning to see the light and they are beginning to see how they can put the blockchain to use to clean up their own acts, to make every transaction accountable and transparent.

As you have seen, the cryptography that secures blockchain technology is complex; having seen how the public and private keys work, you can see how encryption works to keep you safe, to stop the blockchain from being hacked and misused. You can see how hard it is for someone to change any transaction for their own benefit and you can see how any errors are picked up and stopped in their tracks immediately if they happen.

Lastly, you have seen what the blockchain does now and what it can be used for in the real world. This really is only the tiny tip of a very large iceberg; blockchain technology is changing the world as we know it and, as time goes by, more services, more governments, and financial institutions are going to jump on the bandwagon and implement blockchain technologies for various practical applications.

It is time for the world to become accountable for every transaction made, from the smallest purchase right up to major international transactions carried out by government agencies. Blockchain technology is here to stay and is one innovation that the world will not be able to live without in years to come; it is an innovation that has caused a major upset amongst world powers and governments and it will continue to do so for the foreseeable future.

It's time for the future to become transparent, accountable and secure. It's time for the hackers and malicious users to be pushed out, leaving us safe in the knowledge that our money is secure.

We need to embrace change, encourage innovation , and nurture creativity in order to secure a bright and boundless future for generations to come.

You've reach the end. Congrats.

If you enjoyed this book can you leave a quality review on Amazon please see link below..

LINK: http://amzn.to/2sQKeyM

Other books written by Raymond Kazuya

Bitcoin & Cryptocurrencies Guide: Introduction Learn Everything You Need To Know!

LINK: : http://amzn.to/2tRQpyj

LINK: Investing in Etherum Cryptocurrencies
& Profiting Guide

http://amzn.to/2uuGVt9

GLOSSARY

Merkel Tree - A data structure made up of hashes, blockchain, and merkel root. Enabling efficient and secure authentication for transactions, especially large transactions.

Hash - Branch (^) that connects values together and creates a totally unique and new value from the previous existing values. Basically a hash functions serves to takes some input data and creates some output data. It takes the input of any length to create an output of a fixed length.

Cryptography - The practice and study of techniques in secure communication. In essence deciphering codes that have intended messages.

Smart Contracts - procedures that mediate, validate and negotiate performance of a contract.

Hyper Ledger - An open record data base accessible to anyone in the public that verifies the authenticity of a transaction.

Consensus - Agreement among nodes or blockchain networks which validate a transaction.

Logarithms - is the inverse operation to exponentiation. It's like how division is the inverse of multiplication. For example the base of 10 logarithm of 1000 is 3, meaning 10 to the power of 3. Therefore, 10 is used as a factor 3 times.

Algorithms - set of rules that are used to perform complex calculations, usually conducted by a computer.

Encryption - Converting data into a complex code, thus concealing data from unauthorized access.

Authenticate - The process of validating the accuracy of a transaction. Confirming if certain values within a transaction is legitimate or not.

Bitcoin - An intangible cryptocurrency that is used like any other fiat currency to purchase or exchange goods and services. We ascribe value to Bitcoins much like we do the USD or EU.

Diagrams

How the bitcoin exchange process works see below:

Bitcoin

↓

BTC network

↓

Authentication Process

↓

Validation through the Ledger

↓

Consensus via BTC Network

↓

Miners Paid as an Incentive

www.ingramcontent.com/pod-product-compliance
Lightning Source LLC
Chambersburg PA
CBHW060943050326
40689CB00012B/2566

* 9 7 8 1 5 4 8 7 3 6 8 0 4 *